Flav

SOM

RECIPES

C000215212

Compiled by Julia Skinner

THE FRANCIS FRITH COLLECTION

www.francisfrith.com

First published in the United Kingdom in 2013 by The Francis Frith Collection®

This edition published exclusively for Bradwell Books in 2013
For trade enquiries see: www.bradwellbooks.com or tel: 0800 834 920
ISBN 978-1-84589-722-2

Text and Design copyright The Francis Frith Collection®
Photographs copyright The Francis Frith Collection® except where indicated.

The Frith® photographs and the Frith® logo are reproduced under licence from
Heritage Photographic Resources Ltd, the owners of the Frith® archive and trademarks.
'The Francis Frith Collection', 'Francis Frith' and 'Frith' are registered trademarks of
Heritage Photographic Resources Ltd.

British Library Cataloguing in Publication Data

Flavours of Somerset - Recipes
Compiled by Julia Skinner

The Francis Frith Collection
6 Oakley Business Park,
Wylye Road, Dinton,
Wiltshire SP3 5EU
Tel: +44 (0) 1722 716 376
Email: info@francisfrith.co.uk
www.francisfrith.com

Printed and bound in Malaysia
Contains material sourced from responsibly managed forests

Front Cover: **CHARD, COTTAGES 1907** 58768t
Frontispeice: **PORLOCK, HIGH STREET 1919** 69270
Contents: **BURNHAM-ON-SEA, DONKEYS ON THE SANDS 1913** 65384

The colour-tinting is for illustrative purposes only, and is not intended to be historically accurate

CONTENTS

PUNKIE NIGHT

The recipe on the opposite page is not a traditional Somerset one, but was inspired by the Punkie Night celebration that takes place each year at the village of Hinton St George near Crewkerne in South Somerset. 'Punkie' is an old name for the lanterns made from hollowed-out root crops and carved to resemble grotesque faces that are traditionally made at Halloween (31st October) to frighten away goblins, evil spirits and – in Somerset – 'spunkies', the local name for what are called Will-o'-the-Wisps elsewhere. These are small glowing balls of ignited marsh gas that rise from low-lying wetland such as the Somerset Levels. It was believed in Somerset in the past that spunkies were the lost souls of children who had died unbaptised and were presagers of death. In fact, Halloween used to be known as Spunkie Night or Punkie Night in several parts of Somerset, although the Punkie Night celebration at Hinton St George takes place on the last Thursday of October, and is not linked directly with Halloween.

On Punkie Night at Hinton St George the local children parade through the village carrying candle-lit punkie lanterns made from a variety of hollowed-out and intricately-carved root crops, such as turnips, swedes, sugar beets, mangel-wurzels, squashes and pumpkins. They spend many days before Punkie Night making their beautifully designed and very elaborate lanterns, which nowadays are not always in the form of frightening faces. In former times the children went round the village begging for candles to light their lanterns, in the same way that children go 'trick or treating' elsewhere on Halloween. The story goes that the custom originated when the men of the village used to go to the annual fair that was held at this time at Chiselborough, a few miles to the north-east. One year they were so much the worse for wear after their day of jollification that they were unable to find their way back to Hinton, so the women and children of the village made some punkie lanterns and went out into the dark night to round up their drunken menfolk and bring them home.

RECIPE

PUNKIE SOUP

The children of Hinton St George use all sorts of root vegetables to make their punkie lanterns nowadays, but they were originally made with mangel-wurzles (grown for animal fodder) or turnips, as used here to make this surprisingly tasty soup. However, you can use butternut squash instead if you prefer, or perhaps some pumpkin left over from making your own punkie lanterns for Halloween. Serves 6.

450g/1 lb small turnips (about grapefruit-sized),
   peeled and cut into small pieces
225g/8oz potatoes, peeled and cut into small pieces
1 large leek, trimmed, washed and sliced
1 onion, peeled and roughly chopped
50g/2oz butter
2 level tablespoonfuls plain flour
1.8 litres/3 pints chicken or vegetable stock
Salt and freshly ground black pepper

Melt the butter in a large saucepan and add the vegetables. Cover the pan with its lid and cook over a low heat for 15 minutes. Add the flour and cook for a few minutes, stirring continuously. Gradually blend in the stock and season well with salt and pepper. Bring to the boil, then reduce the heat and simmer gently for about 30 minutes, or until the vegetables are tender. Remove from the heat and allow the soup to cool a little before processing it through a blender or liquidizer until smooth. Return the soup to the pan, check the seasoning and re-heat before serving.

'It's Punkie Night tonight,
It's Punkie Night tonight,
Give me a candle, give me a light,
If you don't, you'll get a fright!'

3

RECIPE

SOMERSET CHEESE SOUP

This is an unusual but delicious creamy soup. Serves 4.

> 25g/1oz butter
> 2 medium onions, peeled and roughly chopped
> 4 sticks of celery, trimmed and chopped into small pieces
> 2 level tablespoonfuls plain flour
> ½ teaspoonful dry mustard powder
> 300ml/ ½ pint vegetable or chicken stock
> 600ml/1 pint milk
> Salt and pepper
> 115g/4oz mature, tasty Cheddar cheese, grated
> A little freshly grated nutmeg

Melt the butter in a large pan, add the chopped onions and celery and cook for 10-15 minutes, until softened but not browned. Mix in the flour and mustard powder and cook for 2-3 minutes, stirring continually. Gradually blend in the stock and milk, then bring to the boil, stirring continually. Reduce the heat, cover the pan with its lid and simmer gently for 30-40 minutes, until the vegetables are tender, stirring occasionally so the mixture does not stick to the bottom of the pan. Remove the pan from the heat and allow the mixture to cool slightly, then process it in a blender or liquidizer until smooth, return to the pan and season to taste with salt and pepper and a little freshly grated nutmeg. If necessary, the soup can be prepared in advance up to this point.

When ready to serve, re-heat the soup, stir in the grated cheese and serve immediately.

CHEDDAR GORGE, HIGH ROCK c1873 6984

CHEDDAR CHEESE

Cheddar is a village on the southern edge of the Mendip Hills in Somerset, close to the spectacular Cheddar Gorge, which has given its name to the biggest and probably the most famous British cheese. The process of making Cheddar cheese began on the farms around there many centuries ago – the earliest record of it is from 1170, when the accounts of the royal court show that King Henry II (1154-89) liked Cheddar cheese so much he bought 80 hundredweight of it (4,645kg).

The success of the cheese was due to the quality of the water and rich pasture of the area. The cows that grazed there yielded excellent milk for making the cheese, which originally had to be produced within 30 miles of Wells Cathedral to be classed as 'Cheddar cheese'. To make proper Cheddar cheese, the milk is poured into a large cheese vat, the culture is added, then the curds and whey are separated and the curds are cut into large lumps. The lumps are then constantly turned by hand for an hour until they become flatter and the moisture is lost – this is the process known as Cheddaring, which depends very much on the cheesemaker's skill and experience. The lumps are then broken up by hand and put into cloth-lined moulds. The cheeses are then pressed for a day, then wrapped in muslin and left to mature on wooden shelves in a cool store for at least 3 months, but sometimes much longer. They are turned every day at first, but less frequently as they age. The cheese can be ready to eat after 3 months, when the young cheese will have a sweet and mild taste, but the best Cheddar is left to mature and mellow for a further 9 or even 15 months, when it will have a rich, nutty flavour. The long maturing time produces a rind and allows the gradual change in texture of the cheese to take its effect on flavour development.

CHEDDAR, SALLY SPENCER AND GLEN MIDDLE MILL 1908 60144

The type of cheese made by the Cheddaring process has become so popular that is now made all over the world, and the name 'Cheddar cheese' has no Protected Designation of Origin (PDO) within the European Union. However, only Cheddar produced from local milk within four counties of south-west England – Somerset, Dorset, Devon and Cornwall – may use the name 'West Country Farmhouse Cheddar', whilst truly authentic Cheddar cheese, made the traditional way using local milk, is still made in the village of Cheddar by the award-winning Cheddar Gorge Cheese Company, who also sell their products online: www.cheddargorgecheese.co.uk

CASTLE CARY, THE MARKET PLACE c1955 C611025

This photograph shows the former market hall in the centre of Castle Cary in south Somerset. The town has now expanded to absorb the neighbouring village of Ansford, where the Parsonage was the birthplace in 1740 of James Woodforde. He became a clergyman when he grew up and worked as a curate in Somerset for many years before moving away to Norfolk. He is famous for his diaries, which he kept for nearly 45 years; they have been published as 'The Diary of a Country Parson' and form a fascinating record of life in 18th-century rural England. On the right of this view is the George Inn at Castle Cary which features in several diary entries. One was for July 22nd 1777 when Reverend Woodforde recorded how a crowd had assembled outside the George to see the wretched Robert Biggen lashed to a cart and whipped round the streets of the town for stealing potatoes. There was a collection of seventeen shillings and sixpence for the local hangman – 'an old man and a most villainous looking Fellow' – who did the whipping, but James Woodforde would have none of it: 'For my part, I would not contribute one Farthing to it.'

RECIPE

CHEESE AND POTATO BAKE

This makes a good vegetable accompaniment to serve with a main course, and can also be served as a light supper dish. Serves 4-6.

50g/2oz butter
900g/2 lbs potatoes, peeled
2 medium onions, peeled
600ml/1 pint milk
175g/6oz tasty Cheddar cheese, grated
Salt and freshly ground black pepper
Freshly grated nutmeg

Pre-heat the oven to 170°C/325°F/Gas Mark 3.

Use some of the butter to liberally grease a shallow ovenproof dish. Slice the potatoes and onions as thinly and evenly as possible. Starting with a layer of potato, arrange alternate layers of potato, onion, and grated cheese in the dish, seasoning each layer of potato with salt, pepper and a little freshly grated nutmeg, and dotting it with small knobs of butter. Finish with a layer of potato topped with the remaining cheese. Pour in the milk.

Cover the dish with a tightly fitted piece of kitchen foil and bake in the pre-heated oven for 1½ hours. Remove the foil lid and cook for a further 20-30 minutes, until the potatoes are completely tender and the cheese topping is crisp and bubbling.

RECIPE

LEEKY PIE

Leeks were widely grown in cottage gardens in the past, and feature in many West Country recipes. Leeky Pie was traditionally a dish to serve on high days and holidays.

> 6 medium-sized leeks
> 25g/1oz butter
> 4 rashers of streaky bacon, de-rinded and chopped
>   into small pieces
> Salt and pepper
> 2 eggs
> 150ml/ ¼ pint double cream, the thickest you can get
> 225g/8oz shortcrust, flaky or puff pastry as preferred

Pre-heat the oven to 200°C/400°F/Gas Mark 6, and grease a deep pie or flan dish or tin about 20-24cms (8-9 ins) in diameter.

Wash and trim the leeks and chop them into small pieces. Melt the butter in a large frying pan, add the chopped leeks and sweat them over a medium heat for about 15 minutes, until they are soft and tender. Place layers of cooked leeks with bacon pieces in the pie or flan dish, seasoning to taste with a little salt and plenty of pepper as you go, finishing with a layer of leeks. Beat the eggs with the cream and pour the mixture into the dish over the filling. Stir it in gently, so that it is evenly distributed.

Dampen the edges of the pie dish. Roll out the pastry and fit it over the filling to make a lid, firming the edges down and pinching them to seal them well. Cut two or three crosses in the pastry lid with a sharp knife to allow steam to escape during cooking. Bake in the pre-heated oven for about half an hour, until the pastry is crisp and golden. This is usually served hot, but it is also nice eaten cold.

LUCCOMBE, COTTAGES 1890 23527

RECIPE

ONION PIE WITH SAVOURY CHEESE PASTRY

For the cheese pastry:
225g/8oz plain flour
115g/4oz butter or margarine
½ teaspoonful salt
½ teaspoonful dry mustard
  powder
Pinch of pepper
115g/4oz Cheddar cheese,
  grated
1 egg yolk
1-2 tablespoonfuls water

For the filling:
300ml/ ½ pint milk
1 bay leaf
50g/2oz butter or margarine
3 medium onions
75g/3oz fresh white
  breadcrumbs
2 eggs
Salt and pepper
60ml/2fl oz/3 tablespoonfuls
  double cream
50g/2oz Cheddar cheese, grated

To make the pastry:

Sieve the flour, salt, mustard powder and pepper into a mixing bowl. Rub in the margarine or butter until the mixture resembles fine breadcrumbs and stir in the grated cheese. Beat the egg yolk with 1 tablespoonful of water and use a round-bladed knife to stir it into the flour mixture, adding enough extra water if necessary to form a fairly stiff dough, and knead it lightly until smooth. Roll out the pastry on a lightly floured surface and use it to line a greased flan dish or tin about 22-24cms (9ins) in diameter. Leave to chill in the fridge until needed.

To make the filling:

Put the milk and bay leaf in a saucepan and heat it until just below boiling point. Remove the pan from the heat and leave to infuse until needed. Meanwhile, peel the onions and slice them quite thinly. Melt the butter or margarine in a large saucepan, add the sliced onions and cook over a gentle heat for about 15 minutes, until they are soft and transparent but not browned. Remove the bay leaf from the milk and pour it over the breadcrumbs in a large bowl. Stir in the cooked onions together with the melted fat from the saucepan.

Pre-heat the oven to 190°C/375°F/Gas Mark 5 and place a baking tray in the oven to heat up.

Beat the eggs then stir them into the mixture. Season to taste with salt and pepper, then mix in the cream and pour the mixture into the prepared pastry case. Place the dish or tin on the hot baking tray in the pre-heated oven (this helps the pastry base to cook through) and bake for about 25 minutes, or until the filling is golden brown and set. Remove from the oven and sprinkle the top with the grated cheese, then return to the oven and cook for another 5 minutes or so, until the cheese topping is bubbling and golden brown. Remove from the oven and leave to cool and settle for a few minutes before eating warm, or leave to cool completely and eat cold.

YEOVIL, HENDFORD HILL 1912 64525x

TAUNTON, THE MARKET AND PARADE 1894 34878

TAUNTON TOAST

Think of Somerset and most people immediately associate it with cider, which features in many traditional recipes from the county. The area around Taunton was being advertised as 'cider country' as early as 1584, and for many centuries cider production was a key factor in the local economy. In 1894 over 24,000 acres of land around Taunton were being used as orchards. The Taunton Cider Company was set up in 1921 at Norton Fitwarren to make cider on a commercial basis. The company expanded and was particularly known for Dry Blackthorn cider, but was bought out by Matthew Clark plc in 1995 and commercial cider production was moved from Norton Fitzwarren to Shepton Mallet. More traditional farmhouse-style cider, or 'scrumpy', is still made in Somerset by a number of small-scale producers and is well worth seeking out. The secret of making good cider is in the blending of juice from several varieties of cider apples, many of which go by delightful names such as Slack-ma-girdle, Honey String, Buttery Door, and Poor Man's Profit.

> 4 thick slices of bread
> 50g/2oz butter or margarine
> 1 level tablespoonful English mustard
> 4 tablespoonfuls dry Somerset cider
> 225g/8oz grated strong Cheddar cheese
> Salt and pepper to taste

Serves 4 as a snack, so increase the quantities for more people. Melt the butter in a saucepan over a gentle heat. Stir in the mustard, cider and cheese, and continue stirring until all the cheese has melted and the mixture is smooth and creamy. Season to taste. Toast the bread, then spread the cheese mixture on the slices. Place them under a hot grill until golden brown and bubbling.

In most cider-making counties of England a ceremony called 'wassailing' used to be held in the orchards every winter. The name comes from the Anglo-Saxon words 'Waes Hal', meaning 'good health', and its purpose was to drive away evil spirits from the trees to ensure a good apple crop the next year. A famous wassailing ceremony still takes place each year in Somerset at Carhampton, a few miles east of Minehead, at the Butchers Arms pub, where the date of 1638 in sheep's knucklebones set into the floor of the bar records when the building first became an inn, or more probably a cider house. The ceremony is held in the orchard behind the pub every January 17th, 'Old Twelfth Night' in the old-style Julian Calendar. Villagers form a circle around the largest apple tree, then cider is poured on its roots and pieces of toast soaked in cider are hung in its branches for the robins, who represent the 'good spirits' of the tree. A shotgun is fired overhead to scare away evil spirits and wake up the trees for the spring, and the traditional Carhampton Wassailing Song is sung:

Old apple tree, we wassail thee,
And hoping thou wilt bear,
For the Lord doth know where we shall be
Till apples come another year.
For to bear well, and to bear well,
So merry let us be,
Let every man take off his hat,
And shout to the old apple tree!
Old apple tree, we wassail thee,
And hoping thou wilt bear
Hatfuls, capfuls and three bushel bagfuls,
And a little heap under the stairs –
Hip, Hip, Hooray!

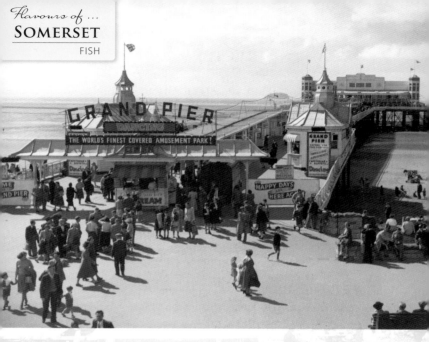

WESTON-SUPER-MARE, THE GRAND PIER c1955 W69079

By the Victorian period the popularity of sea-water bathing led to the development of Somerset's seaside resorts along its Severn Estuary and Bristol Channel coasts, such as Portishead, Clevedon, Weston-super-Mare, Burnham-on-Sea and Minehead. Portishead and Clevedon lie beside the waters of the Severn Estuary, and the Bristol Channel properly begins at Weston-super-Mare – the lower limit of the Severn Estuary and the start of the Bristol Channel is marked by Sand Point, just to the north of the town. The development of these resorts in the 19th century was greatly aided by the arrival of the railways to bring in holidaymakers. Steam trains reached Weston in 1848 and thousands of visitors also came to the resort every year by paddle-steamer, but Weston was just a small fishing village before it developed into the seaside pleasure ground that we know today.

RECIPE

MACKEREL BAKED IN CIDER

This recipe for oven-baked mackerel comes from Somerset, so it is no surprise that it features cider. Serves 4.

  4 mackerel, gutted and cleaned
  Salt and freshly ground black pepper
  75g/3oz butter
  2 dessert apples, peeled, cored and coarsely grated
  1 small onion, peeled and coarsely grated or very
      finely choppped
  200g/7oz Cheddar cheese, grated
  50g/2oz fresh breadcrumbs, brown or white
  60ml/2fl oz/3-4 tablespoonfuls dry cider
  Lemon wedges and finely chopped fresh parsley to garnish

Pre-heat the oven to 180°C/350°F/Gas Mark 4. Butter a wide, shallow ovenproof dish big enough to hold the four mackerel side by side. Melt the butter in a small pan over a low heat and put to one side. Mix together the grated apple, onion, breadcrumbs and 75g (3oz) of the cheese in a bowl and bind with 1 tablespoonful of the melted butter. Season the mackerel inside and out with salt and pepper, then stuff the fish with the breadcrumb mixture and secure the opening of each fish with two or three skewers or cocktail sticks. Place the mackerel side by side in the prepared dish and sprinkle the remaining cheese over each fish. Pour in the remaining melted butter and sufficient cider to cover the base of the dish. Place a piece of buttered kitchen foil or greaseproof paper tightly over the dish as a lid. Bake in the pre-heated oven for 25-35 minutes, until the mackerel are cooked right through and golden brown. Serve straight from the dish and garnish with lemon wedges and parsley.

MINEHEAD, THE BEACH 1906 57157x

Minehead is another popular seaside holiday resort that in earlier
times was a busy fishing community. High on the slopes of North Hill
above the town is its medieval parish church of St Michael. Its tall
tower contains a rood loft with a window where a beacon light used
to be kept burning at night to guide fishing boats home. The tower
contains 10 bells and an old rhyme about their peal goes 'Herring
and bread, go the bells of Minehead', a reminder that from the early
17th century until the late 18th century Minehead was an important
herring fishing port. Its quay was crowded with houses curing 'red
herrings', or kippers, and at the height of the autumn fishing season
Minehead was exporting over 4,000 barrels of salted herrings. Then
the herring shoals in the Bristol Channel disappeared, and purpose-
built herring boats at Minehead had ceased to exist by the early 20th
century.

RECIPE

HERRINGS WITH WALNUT STUFFING

This recipe commemorates the place of herrings in Minehead's history by serving them with a stuffing made with breadcrumbs and walnuts as a tasty supper dish. A few miles west of Minehead are the pretty villages of Bossington and Selworthy, which are famous for their walnut trees. They were originally planted to provide wood for making gunstocks, but their harvest of nuts must also have been very welcome. Serves 4.

> 4 medium herrings, each weighing about 275g/10oz,
>   cleaned, boned and heads and tails removed
> 75g/3oz butter
> 1 medium onion, peeled and very finely chopped
> 50g/2oz fresh wholemeal breadcrumbs
> 50g/2oz shelled walnut pieces, roughly chopped
> 1 tablespoonful English mustard
> Finely grated zest and juice of 1 unwaxed lemon
> 3 tablespoonfuls finely chopped fresh mixed herbs,
>   such as chives, parsley, thyme
> Salt and pepper

Melt 15g/ ½ oz of the butter in a saucepan, add the chopped onion and fry over a gentle heat for about 5 minutes until soft and transparent, stirring occasionally. Mix together the breadcrumbs, walnuts, mustard, lemon rind, mixed herbs and 1 tablespoonful of lemon juice, and season to taste. Add the cooked onion and mix well. Open the herring fillets and lay them skin side down. Press the stuffing mixture evenly over each fillet. Fold the herring fillets back in half and use a sharp knife to slash across the skin several times. Melt the remaining butter in a large, wide frying pan. Add the fish and fry for about 10 minutes, turning them once, until they are tender and browned on each side.

RECIPE

SOMERSET PORK WITH APPLES AND CIDER SAUCE

Use Somerset cider to make a delicious creamy sauce to accompany pork in this recipe.

> 25g/1oz butter
> 500g/1¼ lbs pork tenderloin, cut into small pieces
> 12 baby onions or shallots, peeled and left whole
> 2 teaspoonfuls grated lemon rind
> 300ml/ ½ pint dry cider
> 150ml/ ¼ pint stock
> 2 crisp eating apples, cored and sliced but not peeled
> 3 tablespoonfuls chopped fresh parsley
> 100ml/3½ fl oz whipping cream
> Salt and pepper

Heat the butter in a large sauté or frying pan, and brown the pork in batches. Transfer the pork to a bowl. Add the onions to the pan and cook gently until they are soft. Stir in the lemon rind, cider and stock, increase heat and boil for a few minutes. Return the pork to the pan, reduce heat and cook gently for 25-30 minutes, until the meat is tender. Add the apples to the pan and cook for a further 5 minutes.

Transfer the pork, apples and onions to a warmed serving dish, and keep warm. Stir the cream and parsley into the cooking pan, and allow the sauce to bubble so that it reduces down a bit and thickens slightly. Season to taste, then pour over the pork and serve whilst it is hot.

RECIPE

MENDIP FARM FRY

Belly pork slices are reasonably cheap, so this makes an economical family dish. The pork slices are first fried and then cooked in the oven in a sweet cider sauce, which gives them a delicious flavour. Serves 4.

> 675g/1½ lbs belly pork slices
> 115g/4oz light or dark soft brown sugar
> 450m/ ¾ pint dry cider
> 3 cloves
> Salt and pepper

Put the cider in a pan with the cloves and seasoning, bring to the boil and continue to boil rapidly until the liquid has reduced down to half the original quantity.

Meanwhile, dry-fry the belly pork slices in a frying pan, in two batches if necessary, turning them frequently so they don't stick, until they are lightly browned on both sides. Arrange the slices in one layer in a deep ovenproof or baking dish, and cover them with the brown sugar.

Pre-heat the oven to 200°C/400°F/Gas Mark 6. When the cider is reduced down, take out the cloves and pour the liquid into the dish with the meat. Bake in the pre-heated oven for 30 minutes, then serve with potatoes and seasonal green vegetables with some of the cooking sauce spooned over the meat.

WELLS, THE MARKET PLACE 1890 23894

DAVYS

RECIPE

PRIDDY OGGIES

The Mendip Hills are the carboniferous limestone ridge that runs across Somerset between Weston-super-Mare and Frome. They are veined with traces of 43 minerals including silver and particularly lead, which was mined from the hills from pre-Roman times until the 20th century. A centre of the lead-mining industry was Priddy, whose position at nearly 300 metres (1,000 feet) high on top of the Mendips makes it the highest village in Somerset. 'Oggie' is a West Country name for a pasty. 'Priddy Oggies', with a pork and Cheddar cheese filling, were invented in the 1960s by Mr Paul Leyton at the Miner's Arms pub restaurant at Priddy, and soon became famous. The Miner's Arms is no longer in business, but Priddy Oggies live on as a 'modern' traditional dish from Somerset. This makes 8 oggies.

For the pastry:
25g/1oz butter
25g/1oz lard
1 egg yolk
Half a teaspoonful dry mustard
    powder
115g/4oz Cheddar cheese,
    grated
2½ tablespoonfuls of water
Pinch of salt
225g/8oz plain flour

For the filling:
500g/1¼ lbs pork tenderloin
1 egg, beaten
75g/3oz mature Cheddar
    cheese, grated
2 tablespoonfuls finely
    chopped fresh parsley
Pinch of salt
A pinch of Cayenne pepper
8 rashers of smoked bacon,
    de-rinded

<u>To make the pastry:</u> mix all the ingredients except the flour in a warm bowl until they are soft. Cool the mixture in the fridge until it is firm, then sieve the flour into the cooled mixture and rub it in roughly. Divide the mixture into thirds. Take each piece and roll it 2 or 3 times into a 1cm (½ inch) thick slab. Moisten the top of each slab slightly before laying them all on top of each other. When finished, press down firmly and cut downwards to form three pieces. Repeat the rolling process twice more, then chill for 30 minutes.

<u>To make the filling:</u> trim the pork tenderloin and slice it lengthways into 2 pieces, then beat them gently with a wooden kitchen mallet or rolling pin until each piece is flat and about 5mm (¼ inch) thick. Reserve half the beaten egg, then place the cheese, parsley, salt and cayenne pepper in the bowl with the rest of the egg and mix well. Spread the mixture evenly over the cut sides of the pork, then roll up each piece like a Swiss roll, pressing down firmly. Chill for 30 minutes.

<u>To assemble the oggies:</u> cut each roll of pork into 4 slices and wrap a piece of bacon around each slice. Roll out the pastry and cut it into 8 circles about 15cms (6 ins) in diameter. Lay a slice of the stuffed meat in the centre of each circle of pastry, then moisten around the edges with a little water. Fold the edges of the pastry circles up and over the meat, crimping the edges together firmly to seal them. Put the oggies on a baking sheet, cut a small hole in each one to allow steam to escape during cooking and brush with the remaining beaten egg.

Pre-heat the oven to 200°C/400°F/Gas Mark 6. Bake the oggies in the centre of the oven for 25-30 minutes, until golden brown. (Or an alternative method, as in the earliest form of the recipe, is to part-bake the oggies in the oven for 15 minutes, then deep-fry them until the pastry is crisp and golden).

RECIPE

SOMERSET CROCKY

This is a cross between a hot pot and a pie, with both a potato and a pastry topping, although the pastry lid can be omitted if preferred. As its name suggests, it was originally made in a large earthenware crock or casserole dish. Serves 4-6.

675g/1½ lbs shoulder or leg of lamb, trimmed of fat
   and cut into small pieces
50g/2oz plain flour
3 tablespoonfuls cooking oil
2 onions
450g/1 lb cooking apples
Salt and pepper
600ml/1 pint lamb or beef stock
450g/1 lb potatoes
225g/8oz ready-made puff pastry

Pre-heat the oven to 180°C/350°F/Gas Mark 4. Put the flour in a bowl and season with salt and pepper. Roll the meat pieces in the flour to coat them on all sides. Heat 2 tablespoonfuls of the oil in a large frying pan. Fry the meat in batches for a few minutes in the hot oil until they are browned on all sides, adding the last tablespoonful of oil to the pan towards the end if necessary. Peel and thinly slice the onions and fry in the remaining fat in the pan until they are soft and golden. Peel, core and slice the apples. Arrange the meat, onions and apples in several layers in that order in a large casserole or pie dish, seasoning the meat with salt and pepper. Pour in the stock. Cover the dish with its lid or kitchen foil and cook in the pre-heated oven for 1½ hours or until the meat is tender.

WINSFORD c1960 W112018

Half an hour before the end of the cooking time, peel the potatoes and cut them into thick slices. Bring a pan of salted water to the boil, add the sliced potatoes and parboil them until they are just soft – about 15 minutes – then drain them well. When the meat is ready, remove the dish from the oven, take off the lid and leave for 10 minutes to allow the meat mixture to cool slightly.

Increase the oven temperature to 200°C/400°F/Gas Mark 6. Arrange the potato slices in an overlapping layer on top of the meat. Roll out the pastry and put it on top of the potato layer as a lid, and cut a hole in the pastry to allow steam to escape during cooking. Return the dish to the oven and cook for 25-30 minutes until the pastry is golden brown. (Alternatively, if you don't want to make this with the pastry lid, brush the potato topping with oil or melted butter and cook for 25-30 minutes until they are crisp and golden at the edges).

RECIPE

SOMERSET CHICKEN

This is based on a traditional Somerset recipe for chicken pieces in a tasty sauce. Serve with vegetables and mashed or jacket potatoes, or perhaps the Cheese and Potato Bake on page 9 of this book. Serves 4-6 as necessary.

> 4-6 chicken portions or breasts, with the skin left on
> 50g/2oz butter
> 1 tablespoonful olive oil
> 1 medium onion, peeled and finely chopped
> 75g/3oz button mushrooms, sliced
> 3 level tablespoonfuls plain flour
> 1 level teaspoonful made mustard
> 425ml/ ¾ pint milk
> 150ml/ ¼ pint dry Somerset cider
> 115g/4oz tasty Cheddar cheese, grated
> Salt and freshly ground black pepper
> 1 dessertspoonful finely chopped fresh tarragon leaves

Pre-heat the oven to 200°C/400°F/Gas Mark 6. Season the chicken pieces with salt and black pepper. Melt half the butter in a large frying or sauté pan and add the oil. Cook the chicken pieces in batches for about 2 minutes on each side until they are lightly browned. Put them side by side in an ovenproof dish or deep-sided oven tray and roast in the pre-heated oven for about 30 minutes, until they are cooked right through.

Meanwhile, make the sauce. Melt the remaining butter in the pan the chicken pieces were fried in and cook the chopped onion over a gentle heat until it is soft and transparent, but not browned. Add

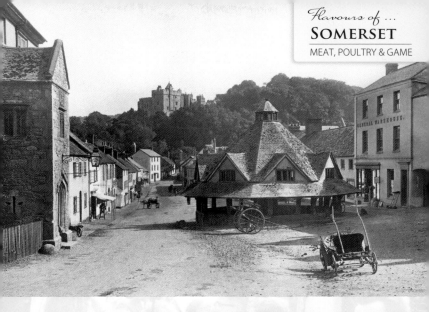

DUNSTER, THE MARKET HOUSE AND CASTLE 1890 27511

the sliced mushrooms and cook for a further minute. Stir in the flour and mustard and cook gently for 2-3 minutes, stirring all the time. Remove the pan from the heat and gradually stir in the milk and cider. Return to the heat and bring to the boil, stirring all the time, until the sauce thickens. Stir in three-quarters of the grated cheese, the chopped tarragon, and salt and pepper to taste. Reduce the heat and simmer gently for five minutes, stirring occasionally so the sauce doesn't stick to the bottom of the pan.

Keep the sauce warm until the chicken pieces are cooked, then pour the sauce over them in the dish. Mix in any cooking juices, and sprinkle the remaining grated cheese over the chicken pieces. Return the dish to the oven for about 10 minutes until the cheese is melted, golden and bubbling, and serve piping hot.

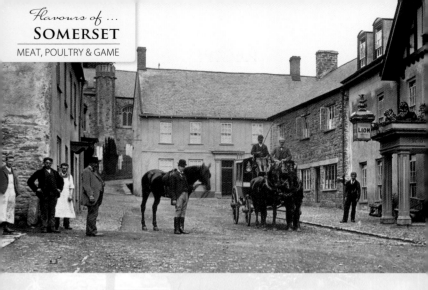

DULVERTON, PEOPLE OUTSIDE THE LION HOTEL 1896 37653x

The beautiful Exmoor National Park straddles the border between
west Somerset and north Devon. It is a wild place of high, rounded
hills and colourful heaths, bright with purple heather and yellow
gorse. Exmoor was a 'royal forest' in medieval times, one of the areas
around the country set aside as a private hunting preserve for the
use of the Norman and medieval kings, and remained so until the
early 1800s, when the area was sold into private hands. Much of the
land was subsequently tamed for agricultural use, especially around
Simonsbath on the extreme western edge of Somerset, but a large
area of Exmoor is still wild moorland, roamed by sheep, semi-wild
Exmoor ponies (although they live rough on the moor all year round,
they all belong to somebody) and the largest number of wild red
deer outside Scotland. The headquarters of the Exmoor National
Park Authority is in the old workhouse at Dulverton, which became
a popular centre for shooting and fishing in the past – at one time,
there were twenty hotels and inns there to cater for visitors.

RECIPE

VENISON CASSEROLE

Use wild venison responsibly sourced from Exmoor in this recipe if possible, but otherwise farmed venison is readily available nowadays in butchers and supermarkets around the country. Venison is a rich and well flavoured meat, low in cholesterol and high in iron. It can sometimes be dry, but a good way of cooking it is in a pot roast, stew or casserole, to make sure it is tender and juicy.

1kg/2 lbs 4oz venison braising steak, cut into cubes
2 tablespoonfuls plain flour, seasoned
50g/2oz butter
2 tablespoonfuls oil
2 onions, peeled and thinly sliced
1 clove of garlic, peeled and finely chopped
600ml/1 pint stock
150ml/ ¼ pint red wine
1 tablespoonful tomato purée
225g/8oz carrots
115g/4oz mushrooms
2 dessertspoonfuls redcurrant jelly
Salt and freshly ground black pepper

Pre-heat the oven to 180°C/350°F/Gas Mark 4. Toss the cubes of venison in the seasoned flour so that all sides are covered. Melt half the butter and oil together in a flameproof casserole that has a tight-fitting lid. Fry the venison, a few cubes at a time, until all sides are browned. Put the browned meat to one side and keep warm. Melt the remaining butter and oil in the casserole, add the sliced onions and cook gently for about 10 minutes, until they are soft and transparent, then add the finely chopped garlic. Stir in the remaining seasoned flour and cook for 1-2 minutes, then add the tomato purée, and then the stock and the red wine, a little at a time, stirring continually. Increase the heat and bring the sauce to the boil, constantly stirring as the sauce thickens. Season to taste with salt and pepper, then add the sliced carrots and mushrooms and the browned venison pieces. Put the lid on the casserole and cook in the pre-heated oven for about 1½ - 2 hours. Stir the redcurrant jelly into the casserole 10 minutes before serving. This casserole is even better if it is made the day before needed, and reheated in the oven before serving.

Flavours of ...
SOMERSET
PUDDINGS, PIES & DESSERTS

RECIPE

WHORTLEBERRY AND APPLE PIE

Whortleberries are small, dark, edible berries that grow wild on Exmoor. They are a form of bilberry (Vaccinium myrtillus), and are also known as worts, hurts or whinberries. They have a delicious flavour and are gathered by local people to make jams, preserves and pies, often teamed with apples, as here, to make a small amount of berries go further. Whortleberries are in season in August and September. They grow on small bushes close to the ground, often hidden under the foliage, and can be hard work to pick, but are worth the effort. However, if you don't want to pick your own whortleberries to make this pie, you can use commercially grown blueberries instead.

    450g/1 lb whortleberries (or blueberries if preferred)
    2 cooking apples
    225g/8oz sugar
    350g/12oz sweet shortcrust or puff pastry, whichever is preferred
    A little milk and extra sugar, to finish

Heat the oven to 200°C/400°F/Gas Mark 6. Remove the cores from the apples with an apple corer, but do not peel them. Stand the apples in an ovenproof dish, add 2 tablespoonfuls of water to the dish and bake in the pre-heated oven for 40-45 minutes, until the apples are tender. When cooked, scrape out the pulp from the apples and mix it with the bilberries and the sugar. Roll out half the pastry on a lightly floured board and use it to line a greased pie tin about 20cms (8 inches) in diameter. Turn out the fruit mixture into the pie tin. Roll out the remaining pastry to make a lid and place it over the pie, trim and seal the edges and cut two holes in the lid for steam to escape during cooking. Brush the lid of the pie with a little milk to glaze, and sprinkle with sugar. Place in the pre-heated oven and bake for ten minutes, then reduce the heat to 180°C/350°F/Gas Mark 4 and cook for a further 30 minutes until the pastry is golden brown and crisp. Serve with custard, cream or ice-cream.

RECIPE

QUANTOCK PUDDING

This recipe for a batter pudding like a large thick pancake studded with blackberries is named after the beautiful Quantock Hills that run from the Vale of Taunton Deane to the Bristol Channel coast east of Watchet. The highest point in the Quantocks is Wills Neck on the hills above the hamlet of Triscombe, north-west of Taunton. Not far away along the ridge of the hillside, beside an old drovers' road along the Quantock Hills, is a small standing stone known as the Triscombe Stone, which is believed to date back to the Bronze Age and probably marked an ancient meeting place. Local legend says that if you sit on the stone and make a wish, it will come true! You can use commercially grown blackberries in this pudding if you prefer, but it's fun to go out into the countryside and forage for wild fruit – and their flavour is much better. Alternatively, you can also make this pudding with blueberries or cherries.

450g/1 lb fresh blackberries
40g/1½ oz butter
50g/2oz plain flour
Pinch of salt
3 eggs, beaten
115g/4oz caster sugar
1 tablespoonful Kirsch fruit brandy or ¼ teaspoonful
   vanilla essence
150ml/ ¼ pint single cream
150ml/ ¼ pint milk

THE QUANTOCKS, TRISCOMBE, WILLS NECK 1929 82112

Pre-heat the oven to 220°C/425°F/Gas Mark 7. Use half the butter
to liberally grease a wide, shallow ovenproof dish of about 1.2
litre (2 pint) capacity. Put the flour, salt and all but 1 tablespoonful
of the sugar in a large bowl. Gradually mix in the beaten eggs,
blending it all together to form a smooth, lump-free batter. Mix in
the Kirsch or vanilla essence, and then the cream and milk. Spread
the blackberries in the dish, pour in the batter and dot small
pieces of the remaining butter all over the top. Bake in the pre-
heated oven for 25-30 minutes, until the batter is puffed up and
golden brown, and set in the centre. Remove from the oven and
leave the pudding to cool down and settle for at least 30 minutes
before sprinkling the top with the remaining sugar and serving it
lukewarm, accompanied with cream.

RECIPE

APPLE DUMPLINGS

Apple Dumplings used to be popular all over the West Country in the past. Using mincemeat for the filling makes this recipe quick and easy, but if you prefer you can make the filling instead with a mixture of 115g/4oz currants, 4 tablespoonfuls of brown sugar, half a teaspoonful of cinnamon or mixed spice and a little lemon juice. Serves 4.

> 4 large cooking apples
> 4 teaspoonfuls mincemeat
> 4 tablespoons brown sugar
> 25g/1oz butter, cut into 4 pieces
> 16 cloves
> 225g/8oz shortcrust pastry
> A little milk to glaze
> Caster sugar, to finish

Pre-heat the oven to 180°C/350°F/Gas Mark 4.

Core the apples, and peel them. Stuff the core hole in each apple with a teaspoonful of mincemeat topped with a tablespoonful of brown sugar (or the filling, as above), and put a small piece of butter on top of the filling. Press 4 cloves into the outside of each apple. Roll out the pastry on a lightly floured surface and cut it into 4 rounds, each big enough to enclose an apple – it is helpful to use an upturned side plate as a guide. Sprinkle each circle with a little caster sugar, and set an apple in the centre.

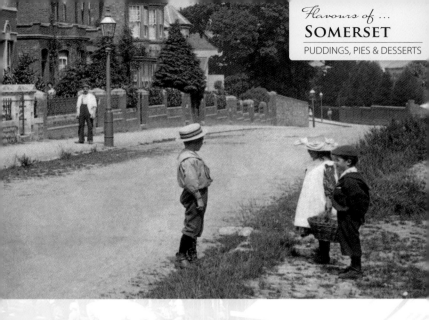

**WELLINGTON, CHILDREN OUTSIDE BLACKDOWN SCHOOL
1907** 58728x

Brush the edges of the pastry rounds with a little water, then
bring up the pastry over each apple to meet at the top, enclosing
it and wrapping it up like a parcel, pressing all the pastry edges
together firmly and smoothing them down well to seal them.
Place the dumplings upside down on a greased baking sheet,
so the top where the sealed edges join is at the bottom, to stop
them coming undone as they cook. Brush the dumplings with
milk and sprinkle with a little caster sugar. Bake in the pre-heated
oven for about 30 minutes, until the pastry is crisp and golden
and the apples are cooked – test by sticking a skewer into one of
the dumplings to make sure the apple is soft. Sprinkle with a little
more caster sugar, and serve hot, with custard or cream.

RECIPE

GLASTONBURY PUDDING

Glastonbury, set on high ground around its famous Tor amid the wetlands of the Somerset Levels, is traditionally associated with the legend of King Arthur as 'Avalon', the 'Island of Apples' of Celtic myth where the king went to die. This delicious steamed pudding is made with a filling of apples and apricots between layers of sponge.

For the sponge:	For the filling:
115g/4oz butter or margarine, softened	1 medium cooking apple, peeled, cored and grated
115g/4oz caster sugar	75g/3oz 'no soak' ready to eat soft dried apricots, finely chopped
2 eggs	
175g/6oz self-raising flour	3 tablespoonfuls apricot jam
Finely grated zest of half an unwaxed lemon	Juice of half a lemon

Grease a pudding basin of 900ml-1.2 litre (1½ -2 pint) capacity. Put all the ingredients for the sponge into a mixing bowl and mix together with an electric whisk or food mixer, or beat by hand with a wooden spoon, until well blended and smooth. Mix together the filling ingredients. Place a layer of the sponge mixture in the pudding basin, then a layer of the filling. Continue filling the basin with alternate layers, finishing with a layer of sponge mixture. Cover the basin with a lid of pleated kitchen foil (to allow room for expansion during cooking), buttered on the pudding side, then a further piece of pleated foil, and tie down firmly with string. Place the basin in the top half of a steamer or a large saucepan filled with boiling water to a third of the way up its side, cover the pan with its lid and steam the pudding for 2 hours, adding more boiling water when necessary to stop it boiling dry. Lift the basin from the pan and leave the pudding to settle in the basin for 5 minutes. Remove the foil lid, run a knife around the inside of the basin to loosen the pudding, then invert it onto a warmed serving dish. Serve with custard or cream.

GLASTONBURY, THE ABBOT'S KITCHEN 1890 23917

Glastonbury's Benedictine abbey was one of the wealthiest and most powerful abbeys in the country in the Middle Ages. Tradition says the abbey was built on the site of the earliest Christian sanctuary in Britain, and it was an important pilgrimage destination in medieval times. Glastonbury Abbey was closed down by King Henry VIII in 1539 as part of his religious reformation and much of its stonework was robbed for re-use in the town, but the ruined remains are impressive and religious services are still held there regularly. The strange building seen in this view was the abbot's kitchen, dating from the 14th century, which is one of the best preserved medieval monastic kitchens in Europe. It was built well away from the main buildings to keep away smoke and cooking smells and reduce the risk of fire, and was designed so that smoke from the four cooking fires in each corner of the building would escape from the openings in the fluted tower at its apex.

RECIPE

BATH GROUND RICE PUDDING

This recipe is similar to a custard tart. It comes from the elegant city of Bath, which was formerly in the historic county of Somerset but is now in the unitary authority of Bath & North East Somerset. Bath is famous for its beautiful Georgian architecture and the hot sulphur springs that issue forth over a quarter of a million gallons of hot water every day. It was the Romans who first developed a health resort town there in the 1st century AD, building a sumptuous complex of hot spring-fed baths that can still be seen today. Bath reached its heyday as a successful inland spa and fashionable social centre in the 18th century under the reign of Richard 'Beau' Nash, the resort's Master of Ceremonies from 1704 to 1761. It was rebuilt and greatly expanded during this period, creating a city that is one of the finest architectural achievements of its age and is particularly renowned for its magnificent crescents. The city of Bath is now designated a UNESCO World Heritage Site.

> 250g/9oz shortcrust pastry (if making your own,
>   use 175g/6oz flour and 75g/3oz fat)
> 300ml/ ½ pint single cream
> 300ml/ ½ pint milk
> 50g/2oz ground rice (you will find this near the pudding rice
>   on supermarket shelves)
> 25g/1oz sugar
> 25g/1oz butter
> 2 eggs, beaten
> 1 teaspoonful sherry, or a few drops of vanilla essence if preferred
> Freshly grated nutmeg

Pre-heat the oven to 190°C/375°F/Gas Mark 5. Grease a flan tin or dish 20-24cms (8-9ins) in diameter and line it with the rolled-out pastry. Line the pastry case with a piece of greaseproof paper or kitchen foil, fill with baking beans and bake it blind for 10 minutes. Remove the beans and paper or foil and cook for another 5 minutes to dry out the base. Remove from the oven, then reduce the oven temperature to 160°C/325°F/Gas Mark 3, and place a baking tin in the oven to heat up.

Put the milk and cream in a saucepan, sprinkle in the ground rice and sugar, and cook in a double boiler (stand the pan inside a larger pan half filled with boiling water, over heat), stirring or whisking with a balloon whisk all the time, until the mixture thickens. Reduce the heat and simmer, stirring, for five minutes. Remove from the heat and leave to cool for a few minutes, then stir in the butter until it is melted and mixed in. Leave to cool for another five minutes before stirring in the beaten eggs and sherry or vanilla essence. Pour the mixture into the pastry case and stand the tin on the hot baking tray in the oven (this helps the pastry base cook through). Bake in the oven at the reduced temperature for 30-40 minutes, until the filling is risen, set in the middle and firm to the touch. Grate a little nutmeg over the top and leave the pudding to settle for about 10 minutes (when the filling will sink down) before serving warm, or this is also very good eaten cold.

BATH, LANSDOWN CRESCENT 1896 38366

RECIPE

SALLY LUNNS

'No more I heed the muffin's zest,
The yeast cake or the bun.
Sweet muse of pastry, teach me how
To make a Sally Lunn.'
(From the Bath Chronicle of 1796)

The oldest house in Bath is at 4 North Parade Passage, formerly Lilliput Alley, behind Bath Abbey. The building currently houses Sally Lunn's tearooms which are named after a French Huguenot refugee called Sally Lunn (her real name was probably Solange Luyon) who took over its lease in 1680. She became famous for the rich, light brioche-type cakes and buns she made there using the baking skills she brought with her from her homeland, and they have continued to be made and sold in Bath ever since. The authentic recipe for the Sally Lunn buns made at Sally Lunn's tearooms is a closely guarded secret, so this is an approximation. This amount should make 6-8 small Sally Lunn buns, depending on the size of your baking rings.

For the yeast batter:
75g/3oz strong white breadmaking flour
1 teaspoonful caster sugar
2 rounded teaspoonfuls easy bake dried yeast (or 1x 7g sachet)
250ml/9fl oz milk, warmed to lukewarm

For the dough:
225g/8oz strong white breadmaking flour
25g/1oz caster sugar
25g/1oz butter, melted and allowed to cool slightly
1 egg, beaten

Place the flour, sugar and yeast for the batter into a large mixing bowl. Gradually blend in the warmed milk until a smooth batter is formed. Cover with a damp cloth or put the bowl inside a polythene bag and leave in a warm place for 30 minutes until it is frothy. When the batter is ready, sift in the flour from the dough ingredients, add the sugar, melted butter and beaten egg, and mix to form a gloopy dough. Cover and leave again in a warm place for 1½ -2 hours until the dough has risen and doubled in size. Turn the dough out onto a lightly floured surface and knead it gently for a few seconds until it is smooth, sprinkling it with just a little extra flour if necessary, if it is still very sticky.

Grease 6-8 metal baking rings about 10-12cms (4-4½ ins) in diameter, such as very small cake tins, crumpet rings or large metal biscuit cutters, and stand them on a greased baking tray. Shape the dough into 6-8 small balls and put one into each tin or ring. Cover and leave again for 30-45 minutes to rise.

Pre-heat the oven to 200°C/400°F/Gas Mark 6. Bake the buns in the pre-heated oven for about 15 minutes until they have risen and their tops are golden brown and firm when pressed.

Split the Sally Lunn buns in half, spread them with thick or whipped cream and perhaps jam, put the halves back together and eat whilst they are still warm. They can also be eaten like teacakes, split in half and toasted, buttered and spread with jam and cream. Alternatively, they can also be split in half, toasted and spread with savoury fillings, or perhaps topped with a fried or poached egg.

Flavours of ...
SOMERSET
TEATIME & BAKING

Grape=Nuts

Rowntree's
ELECT COCOA

Rowntree's
ELECT COCOA

H.R. HUGHES

RECIPE

APPLE CAKE

Crumbly Apple Cake is popular all over the West Country, although there is some argument about whether it should include dried fruit or not. It is traditionally eaten with thick cream, either cold as a cake or hot from the oven as a delicious pudding.

225g/8oz self-raising flour
1 heaped teaspoonful baking powder
½ teaspoonful ground cinnamon or mixed spice
115g/4oz butter or margarine
450g/1 lb cooking apples, peeled, cored and chopped
   into small pieces
115g/4oz soft brown or caster sugar
50g/2oz raisins and/or sultanas (optional)
1 egg
1 tablespoonful milk
A little extra sugar to sprinkle on top – caster or demerara
   as preferred.

Pre-heat the oven to 190°C/375°F/Gas Mark 5 (slightly less for a fan oven) and grease and line a round cake tin about 18-20cms (7-8 ins) in diameter.

Sift the flour, baking powder and spice into a bowl. Rub in the butter or margarine then add the chopped apple, sugar and dried fruit, if using. Beat the egg with the milk, and add to the mixture. Mix together well – it may seem quite stiff, but the apples will cook down to form a moist cake. Turn the mixture into the prepared cake tin, smooth the top and sprinkle with the extra sugar. Bake just below the centre of the pre-heated oven for about 45 minutes, until the top of the cake is golden brown and firm when you gently press down on it. Leave to cool in the tin for 15 minutes then turn out on to a wire rack to cool completely, if eating as a cake, and store in an airtight tin.

Shepton Mallet is a centre of modern commercial cider making nowadays, where the Gaymer Cider Company is the second largest cider maker in the world. In past centuries cider played a massive part in the rural economy, and many agricultural workers received part of their wages in cider made on the farm. The traditional farmhouse cider that is still made in Somerset is famously potent stuff, so strong in fact that it helped cause the resignation of the 1st Lord of the Treasury in the 18th century! In 1763 the British government had reached unprecedented levels of national debt following the country's involvement in the Seven Years War. In an attempt to solve the problem Lord Bute tried to introduce the Cider Bill to put a tax on the production of cider, having realised this would produce a huge increase in revenue from rural areas. There was widespread outrage against the bill which triggered Cider Riots all over the West Country but particularly in Somerset, and Lord Bute became so unpopular he had to step down from office. Sadly for the cider producers and drinkers, his successor, George Grenville, managed to get the bill through Parliament.

RECIPE

CIDER CAKE

When making this cake, remember to soak the dried fruit in cider in good time before you need it – this makes the fruit lovely and juicy, resulting in a deliciously moist and tasty cake.

225g/8oz mixed sultanas, raisins and currants
150ml/5 fl oz/ ¼ pint cider
175g/6oz butter or margarine, softened to room temperature
175g/6oz soft brown sugar
3 eggs, beaten
225g/8oz self-raising flour (either white or wholemeal works well)
1 teaspoonful mixed spice

Soak the dried fruit in the cider overnight, or at least 12 hours before making this cake.

Pre-heat the oven to 180°C/350°C/Gas Mark 4. Grease a 20-24cm (8-9 inch) round or square cake tin and line it with greaseproof paper.

Cream the butter or margarine, add the sugar and cream until light and fluffy. Lightly beat the eggs and gradually beat them into the mixture, a little at a time, adding a spoonful of flour to prevent curdling. Stir in the soaked dried fruit and remaining cider. Add the flour and mixed spice, mix thoroughly and beat well. Pour the mixture into the prepared tin and bake just below the centre of the pre-heated oven for about 1 hour and 10 minutes, until the surface is risen and firm to the touch, and a skewer inserted into the middle comes out clean – cover the top with a piece of kitchen foil or greaseproof paper if it seems to be browning too quickly. Leave to settle in the tin for 5 minutes, then turn out onto a wire rack to cool completely.

BRIDGWATER, THE CORNHILL 1936 87453

In Anglo-Saxon times Somerset was part of the kingdom of Wessex.
A famous king of Wessex was King Alfred the Great, who ruled from
AD871 until 899. He fought a long struggle against the Viking Danes
who were overrunning his kingdom, and in AD878, on the brink
of defeat, he retreated to a stronghold in the marshy area around
Athelney in Somerset to regroup his forces. In the spring of that year
King Alfred summoned all the fighting men of Wessex to meet him at
'the stone of Egbert in the eastern part of the wood called Selwood',
near what is now Penselwood, north-east of Wincanton, for one last
push against the Danes. King Alfred and his army then marched to
Wiltshire where they defeated the Danes at the Battle of Edington.
The area of Somerset where King Alfred took refuge is in Sedgemoor,
the low-lying area that runs across the coastal plain and inland area of
central Somerset. The administrative centre and largest settlement of
Sedgemoor is Bridgwater, where the heart of the town is the domed
building in the background of this view, which was constructed in
1834 to house its indoor market.

RECIPE

SEDGEMOOR EASTER CAKES

It was during his time hiding in the Somerset marshes that the famous legend of King Alfred burning the cakes is set. King Alfred had taken shelter in the cottage of a peasant woman who was unaware of his true identity. She left him to watch a batch of cakes she had set to cook near the fire whilst she went outside to do some chores, but the king was so deep in thought about his problems that he forgot to watch them and let them burn. When the woman returned, she berated him soundly! These thick fruited biscuits are known as cakes in the West Country, and were traditionally baked at Easter time. There are several recipes for them, but this version comes from the Sedgemoor region of Somerset. This should make 18 Easter Cakes, but don't follow King Alfred's example and let them burn!

225g/8oz plain flour
A pinch of salt
½ teaspoonful ground cinnamon
½ teaspoonful mixed spice
115g/4oz butter, softened
115g/4oz caster sugar
75g/3oz currants
1 egg
2 tablespoonfuls brandy

Pre-heat the oven to 180°C/350°F/Gas Mark 4. Grease 2 baking sheets, or line with baking paper. Sieve the flour, salt, cinnamon and mixed spice into a bowl. Rub in the butter, then mix in the sugar and currants. Beat the egg with the brandy, and stir into the mixture to form a dough. Knead the dough gently until it is smooth and soft, then roll it out to about 1cm (half an inch) thick and cut into small rounds with a fluted biscuit cutter 6.5cms (2½ ins) in diameter. Arrange the rounds on the baking sheets and bake in the pre-heated oven for 15-20 minutes, until they are crisp and golden but not over-browned. Remove from the oven and leave the rounds on the baking sheets for five minutes to settle and firm up, then transfer to a wire rack to cool.

FRANCIS FRITH

PIONEER   VICTORIAN   PHOTOGRAPHER

Francis Frith, founder of the world-famous photographic archive, was a complex and multi-talented man. A devout Quaker and a highly successful Victorian businessman, he was philosophical by nature and pioneering in outlook. By 1855 he had already established a wholesale grocery business in Liverpool, and sold it for the astonishing sum of £200,000, which is the equivalent today of over £15,000,000. Now in his thirties, and captivated by the new science of photography, Frith set out on a series of pioneering journeys up the Nile and to the Near East.

INTRIGUE AND EXPLORATION

He was the first photographer to venture beyond the sixth cataract of the Nile. Africa was still the mysterious 'Dark Continent', and Stanley and Livingstone's historic meeting was a decade into the future. The conditions for picture taking confound belief. He laboured for hours in his wicker dark-room in the sweltering heat of the desert, while the volatile chemicals fizzed dangerously in their trays. Back in London he exhibited his photographs and was 'rapturously cheered' by members of the Royal Society. His reputation as a photographer was made overnight.

VENTURE OF A LIFE-TIME

By the 1870s the railways had threaded their way across the country, and Bank Holidays and half-day Saturdays had been made obligatory by Act of Parliament. All of a sudden the working man and his family were able to enjoy days out, take holidays, and see a little more of the world.

With typical business acumen, Francis Frith foresaw that these new tourists would enjoy having souvenirs to commemorate their days out. For the next thirty years he travelled the country by train and by pony and trap, producing fine photographs of seaside resorts and beauty spots that were keenly bought by millions of Victorians. These prints were painstakingly pasted into family albums and pored over during the dark nights of winter, rekindling precious memories of summer excursions. Frith's studio was soon supplying retail shops all over the country, and by 1890 F Frith & Co had become the greatest specialist photographic publishing company in the world, with over 2,000 sales outlets, and pioneered the picture postcard.

FRANCIS FRITH'S LEGACY

Francis Frith had died in 1898 at his villa in Cannes, his great project still growing. By 1970 the archive he created contained over a third of a million pictures showing 7,000 British towns and villages.

Frith's legacy to us today is of immense significance and value, for the magnificent archive of evocative photographs he created provides a unique record of change in the cities, towns and villages throughout Britain over a century and more. Frith and his fellow studio photographers revisited locations many times down the years to update their views, compiling for us an enthralling and colourful pageant of British life and character.

We are fortunate that Frith was dedicated to recording the minutiae of everyday life. For it is this sheer wealth of visual data, the painstaking chronicle of changes in dress, transport, street layouts, buildings, housing and landscape that captivates us so much today, offering us a powerful link with the past and with the lives of our ancestors.

Computers have now made it possible for Frith's many thousands of images to be accessed almost instantly. The archive offers every one of us an opportunity to examine the places where we and our families have lived and worked down the years. Its images, depicting our shared past, are now bringing pleasure and enlightenment to millions around the world a century and more after his death.

For further information visit: www.francisfrith.com

INTERIOR DECORATION

Frith's photographs can be seen framed and as giant wall murals in thousands of pubs, restaurants, hotels, banks, retail stores and other public buildings throughout Britain. These provide interesting and attractive décor, generating strong local interest and acting as a powerful reminder of gentler days in our increasingly busy and frenetic world.

FRITH PRODUCTS

All Frith photographs are available as prints and posters in a variety of different sizes and styles. In the UK we also offer a range of other gift and stationery products illustrated with Frith photographs, although many of these are not available for delivery outside the UK – see our web site for more information on the products available for delivery in your country.

THE INTERNET

Over 100,000 photographs of Britain can be viewed and purchased on the Frith web site. The web site also includes memories and reminiscences contributed by our customers, who have personal knowledge of localities and of the people and properties depicted in Frith photographs. If you wish to learn more about a specific town or village you may find these reminiscences fascinating to browse. Why not add your own comments if you think they would be of interest to others? See **www.francisfrith.com**

PLEASE HELP US BRING FRITH'S PHOTOGRAPHS TO LIFE

Our authors do their best to recount the history of the places they write about. They give insights into how particular towns and villages developed, they describe the architecture of streets and buildings, and they discuss the lives of famous people who lived there. But however knowledgeable our authors are, the story they tell is necessarily incomplete.

Frith's photographs are so much more than plain historical documents. They are living proofs of the flow of human life down the generations. They show real people at real moments in history; and each of those people is the son or daughter of someone, the brother or sister, aunt or uncle, grandfather or grandmother of someone else. All of them lived, worked and played in the streets depicted in Frith's photographs.

We would be grateful if you would give us your insights into the places shown in our photographs: the streets and buildings, the shops, businesses and industries. Post your memories of life in those streets on the Frith website: what it was like growing up there, who ran the local shop and what shopping was like years ago; if your workplace is shown tell us about your working day and what the building is used for now. Read other visitors' memories and reconnect with your shared local history and heritage. With your help more and more Frith photographs can be brought to life, and vital memories preserved for posterity, and for the benefit of historians in the future.

Wherever possible, we will try to include some of your comments in future editions of our books. Moreover, if you spot errors in dates, titles or other facts, please let us know, because our archive records are not always completely accurate—they rely on 140 years of human endeavour and hand-compiled records. You can email us using the contact form on the website.

Thank you!

For further information, trade, or author enquiries
please contact us at the address below:

The Francis Frith Collection, 6 Oakley Business Park, Wylye Road, Dinton, Wiltshire SP3 5EU England.
Tel: +44 (0)1722 716 376 Fax: +44 (0)1722 716 881
e-mail: sales@francisfrith.co.uk **www.francisfrith.com**